Relative Genius:

Lost in Transition

Real life examples of the crazy things adults say that will have you laughing out loud

By Ron Lang

Copyright © 2019 Ron Lang All rights reserved.

No part of this publication may be reproduced, distributed, or transmitted in any form without the prior written permission of the publisher.

Exceptions only apply with small samples to be used specifically for reviews, when recommending the work for others' enjoyment, and certain other non-commercial attempts for laughs as permitted by copyright law.

Please Note: All the principles' names have been omitted or changed to protect the not so innocent and those associated.

Print ISBN-13: 978-1-7338893-0-8

Ebook ISBN-13: 978-1- 7338893-1-5

This book is dedicated to my mother, Susette, who encouraged me to write and produce it. Despite life's difficulties, we always seemed to find something to laugh about. You had a wonderful smile, and we all miss you!

Table of Contents

Introduction .... - 1 -
Quotes of Relative Genius .... - 3 -
Bonus Stories .... - 171 -
Acknowledgements .... - 179 -
About the Author .... - 181 -

Introduction

There is too much seriousness and negativity in the world. Wouldn't it be more bearable if we could laugh a little more? The funniest things can't be scripted. Often, the spontaneous things adults say or do make us scratch our heads or laugh out loud. Relative Genius is full of examples. My wife and I always share laughs about the funny things we have experienced. Many times, we would share them with others for fun, and it usually turned into an impromptu stand-up act. Invariably, I seemed to forget some, so I started writing them down. My mom always enjoyed hearing the stories and knew that others would as well, so she suggested that I convert them into book form.

The quotes throughout this book are actual things that adults have said of their own volition. I have masked the participants' names, but have maintained accuracy in the details of the stories and quotes. Now, you can be in on the joke! There are plenty of things that will make you laugh and brighten your day. Read it for five minutes after work to de-stress. Invite your friends to join you for drinks and samples of the book. Or, you can savor it in private, without the risk of bursting with laughter in front of others. A smile will cross your face, and you will certainly find some gems that you'll want to share with others. All of it is here waiting for you, so turn the page and enjoy!

Quotes of Relative Genius

Andy told his friend that his oldest son was going back to jail for violating his probation. When asked why, Andy said that his son hadn't done anything wrong. Trying to be supportive, the friend asked why they would put him in jail without any evidence. Andy replied:

"They didn't believe him because he failed a Polygrip test."

*He makes a good point. How can you lie through your teeth when you can't even keep your teeth securely in your mouth?

Joan was talking to her younger sister, Ally, about her boyfriend Sean's promotion. Sean worked in the kitchen area at a restaurant chain, and this is a portion of the conversation:

Joan: "Sean just got promoted at work."

Ally: "Good for him. What will he be doing now?"

Joan: "He now has the title of Colonary Specialist."

Ally: "No Joan, that is not his title."

Joan: "Yes it is. He is my boyfriend. I think I would know that he was just promoted to Colonary Specialist!"

Ally: "You are stupid. It is culinary, not colonary!"

*That is a reminder for me not to eat at that restaurant chain!

Tony left work and headed to the hospital to visit his sick mother-in-law. As he was walking in, he bumped into Martin, an old friend from high school. Martin told him that his mother had been in and out of the hospital. When Tony asked how she was currently doing, Martin reported:

"Not too good. The just put her on a breathalyzer!"

*So that you know, Martin's mother was not in the hospital because of any alcohol-related illness.

Jill, an engineer, called Lorena to get some specifications for a project that she was working on. Lorena had a busy schedule and started rattling off the desired information. Jill was having a hard time transposing all the numbers, so she told Lorena:

"Slow down, you know that I am a little O.C.D.C."

*She must have meant that she has OCD, or she was trying to say that her radio was playing ACDC so loud that she couldn't hear the information.

A couple had moved to a new town. The woman was talking with her mother about how they were acclimating to the new community. She told her mother that they found a church that they really liked. She explained to her mother that the Pastor was very direct, and this is how she described him:

"He is one of those fire and rhinestone preachers!"

* I am sure those were some interesting sermons (and outfits for that matter)!

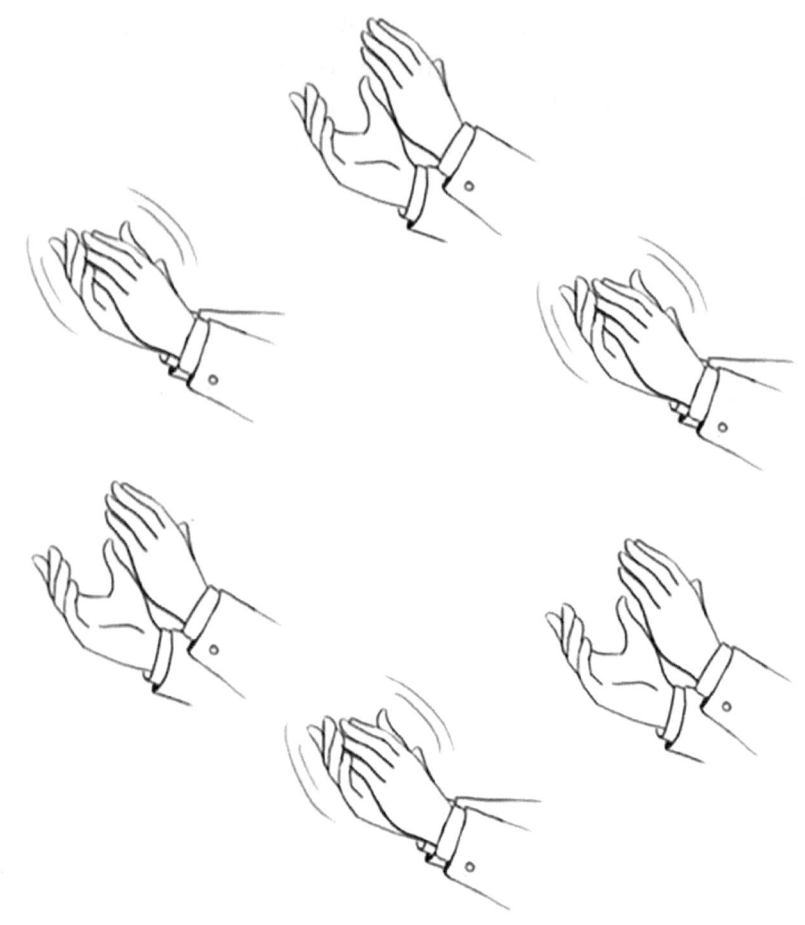

Lisa has done public speaking for many years. At a relative's wedding reception, she was asked to introduce the wedding party. As she completed the first introduction, she urged the audience:

"Let's give them a round hand of applause"

She repeated it after introducing each couple!

I was at the grocery store, and there was a lady in the aisle talking very loudly on her cell phone. Although I wasn't trying to hear her conversation, she made it difficult to ignore. She said something that sounded funny to me, but I thought that couldn't have been what she said. Fortunately, the person on the phone asked her to repeat it, and this is the resulting conversation between the two:

"Hoe and below, he showed up there too."

The person, she was talking to, must have asked her to say it one more time, because this is what I heard next:

"Yeah, hoe and below. You've never heard that before?"

Before I moved to the next aisle, I heard this:

"Low and behold?........ Are you sure?"

An elderly lady was having trouble breathing, so her daughter called an ambulance. When the EMS team arrived, the elderly woman told them that she was feeling better. They wanted to evaluate her and make sure she was going to be okay. When asked what happened, the woman simply stated:

"I was watching the news and just got overwhammed."

* With everything on the news today, I can understand how she would become so overwhelmed!

Amy came home from the gym to find her roommate, Rosie, searching around their apartment. Amy asked what she was trying to find. Rosie told her that she couldn't find her keys, which prompted Amy to help look for the missing set. All of a sudden, Amy began reciting "K...E...Y...S...keys". A confused Rosie inquired what good the chant would do, to which Amy assuredly replied:

"You know what they say; Speak and you shall find!"

*W...I...N...N...I...N...G......L...O...T...T...E...R...Y......T...I...C...K...E...T......
........Winning Lottery Ticket! ....

Oh well, I guess that doesn't work very well.

Two friends were having lunch and laughing about jokes that they had been sent via e-mail. Benji pulled up a joke on his phone and told his friend that he had to read it. Clayton replied:

"I can't read it without my seeing eye glasses."

During a local newscast, they went live to a news reporter at the location of a holiday parade. She was a young and very excited reporter. It was funny to see her being so excited about the parade, but then she reported:

"We can't wait to see all the blimps!"

* I wonder if it was a derogatory comment about the size of people in attendance or if it was an aerial parade sponsored by a tire company.

A friend was helping Keith make decisions with his company's retirement plan. Keith did not know all the details, so he asked a co-worker to come into his office to help answer the questions. Keith introduced his friend, and explained:

"He is trying to help me set up my retirement. I don't know all the answers, so we wanted to poke your brain for a minute."

* Picking someone's brain can be risky, but poking their brain is downright dangerous.

Dante had been very busy with work and personal situations. He was discussing how he wasn't getting any rest, and it was really taking a toll on him. He told his compassionate friends:

"I am burning three ends of the candle."

*I don't want to know what kind of deformed candle he was using.

Jerry had been to the doctor earlier in the week, and he had been prescribed some medication. A few days later he was visiting his family, when he told them that he needed to go pick up his medication. They inquired why he needed medication. He told them that it was for:

"Rectal Dysfunction"

Figuring that he was constipated, a family member suggested an over-the-counter laxative. Jerry knew that something was amiss, but tried to change the subject to a less private issue.

*Why private? Because he meant that the medication was for erectile dysfunction!

A family had gathered for a vigil at a hospital where a family member was ill. Many of the them were sitting in the lobby together. One of the children noticed a sign that was describing "Sepsis". The child asked her mother what sepsis meant. The mother confidently explained:

"Sepsis is a serious infuction."

*As most of you can tell, the mother wasn't infected with a clear understanding of sepsis.

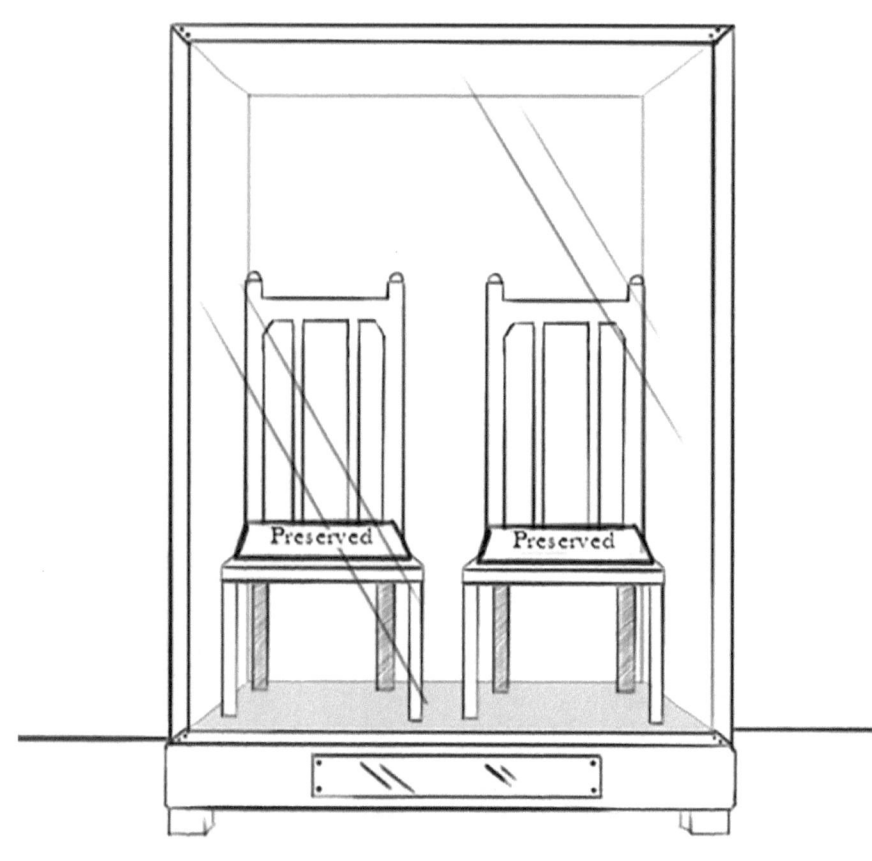

On our way to a graduation ceremony, my wife received a call requesting that we:

"...preserve a couple of seats."

Adam was telling a friend about his family dispute. He believed that he was being helpful, but his family thought otherwise. They were fairly upset with him. Adam explained all the events to his attentive friend and concluded:

"...Now, they are infused with me!"

*Isn't is infuriating when people misunderstand your efforts?

A lady was explaining to a couple about her friend who had been diagnosed with an illness that day. The conversation progressed to them asking if there was anything that they could do to help. The lady told them that there wasn't anything at the moment, because her friend was going to get:

"a reference to another doctor"

They reassured her that they would be supportive in any way they could. She appreciated it, and told them that the path would be clearer once:

"she gets referenced to the other doctor"

*No one could tell if her friend was going to get referred for a second opinion or if she was in search of a reference for employment in the medical industry.

Clive, a salesman, went by Mariko's office attempting to get her to buy one of his services. She wasn't ready to purchase anything, but Clive was very resilient. He kept transitioning to another service that he felt he could get her to buy. There was a question about one of the features, but Clive wasn't sure of the answer. He told Mariko that he would have to get back to her with the correct answer. His reasoning for that reply:

"I don't want to double guess myself!"

A family friend asked the siblings how their mother was doing. The elderly mother had recently begun going to water aerobics. They were all excited for her to start becoming more active and doing it in a social environment. When that friend saw the elderly woman recently, he told her that he was proud of her efforts and asked how she liked it. She told him that it was fine, but she did have some objections. Those objections included that the "old" women gossip too much and...

"...they put too much Clorox in the pool."

*I know that chlorine serves a good purpose in a public pool, but did the maintenance staff also feel that the community needed help brightening their bathing suits?

A very upset woman went into her bank complaining that her debit card was not working. She explained to the bank employees that there hadn't been any problems all morning until she went to buy groceries. In the checkout line, at the grocery store, the card did not work. She told the bankers:

"It kept saying that my card was reclined."

They attempted to help her find the reason behind the card failure, so they asked if she typed in her pin properly. She frustratingly replied:

"All I know is that they reclined my card!"

*Our debit cards should never take a day off!

One evening, a bored husband found himself caught watching an awards show with his wife. He asked himself why he was watching people that he didn't know thanking a bunch of other people that he didn't know. Finally, he was rewarded for his attention. A celebrity, that he didn't recognize, won a particular category. The recipient then began talking about the long journey to this recognition. The recipient told everyone watching across America:

"You guys don't know how bad it was in the beginning. I was at the lowest bottom of the totem pole."

A group of men were at a party debating who they thought was the best college football team. Brent began his arguments with confidence that his opinion was the most accurate. After listening to some compelling points from Rod, Brent changed the direction of his argument. The group, sensing Brent's indecision, began to turn against him. Brent wasn't going to surrender his position easily and said:

> "Rod's points don't even make sense; they are all contrajectory!"

*It didn't matter if Rod's points were contradictory or not. The trajectory of Brent's claim didn't hit the mark with the group.

With a few staff members out sick, a group of employees were pulling together to get all the work completed. Since there wasn't time for the staff to go out to lunch, the manager had lunch delivered. One of the ladies couldn't eat all that she ordered and commented:

"My eyes must have been bigger than my mouth."

* Well, no manager wants an employee with a big mouth.

Jonah and his pal Braxton were discussing their thoughts on the idea of diminished morals in our country. The discussion soon led to the topic of religion. They both believed that a lack of religion in schools was partly to blame for the lack of morals. Jonah expressed his feelings by stating:

"I went to Provochial school, and that's where I learned the differences between right and wrong."

*Parochial school certainly didn't provoke him into a much better education!

A banker went to lunch with her friend from another branch. She had just gone through an audit, and her friend asked her how it had gone. She seemed nonchalant about the experience, and told her friend:

"They wanted to make sure all the T's were T's and all of the I's were I's."

*I suppose that the T's can't be T's unless they are crossed, and the I's have to be dotted to be I's.

A girl was telling her family about a terrible accident that her friends had been in the night before. She explained:

"The accident was so bad that my friend was ejaculated from the vehicle."

*How else would you want to go?

An extended family usually spent Saturday mornings having breakfast together. One of the brothers called his sister and said that he would arrive a little late. She asked him if he wanted them to order something for him, and he requested:

"A hamlet"

She asked him what he meant, and his next answer was:

"It has eggs, cheese, and ham."

She finally asked if he meant that he wanted a ham omelet.

"Yes, that's what I want."

* I am glad that they figured it out, because it would have been a true tragedy to have the waitress read him Shakespeare.

Ashley was a favorite of the office, and it happened to be her birthday. Her colleagues decided to throw a surprise party after their daily meeting. As the meeting was coming to a close, the support staff burst in with a cake and party favors. Everyone was having a good time, and Ashley was very appreciative. Jud, the owner of the business, decided to say a few words about the birthday girl. He attempted to show a negative correlation between her small physical size and her big personality. He began with these words:

"Ashley may be small in statute, but she is all heart!"

* I have never heard that being small in stature was a violation of any statutes, or even office policies.

A father was venting to his wife about how their teenage boys had become more and more rebellious. He was growing more and more frustrated with the neglect of their responsibilities. He felt that talking to them would no longer be effective. He explained this to his wife by exclaiming:

"Everything I say to them just falls on death ears."

* Does a death ear look anything like cauliflower ear?

A guy was telling his nephews how he prepared for football season when he was in high school. The nephews explained that they didn't need any more pointers because they had been following a conditioning program all summer. The uncle, feeling shunned, quipped:

"I am just trying to help. The point of the bottom line is that I have done it before."

* The bottom line is that they didn't want his assistance. That was the point. Period!

Walking out of a movie theater, a husband asked his wife if she was hungry. She answered him by saying:

"The feeling is coming onto me."

He didn't miss a beat and responded:

"As long as I am the one you go to dinner with."

Two cousins were discussing a wedding that one of them had recently attended. The conversation turned to the meal served at the wedding. The lady told her cousin that the meal was decent, but expanded by saying:

"I really liked the vegetable melody."

* All I can picture is a public service announcement where people are dressed as vegetables and singing about eating healthy.

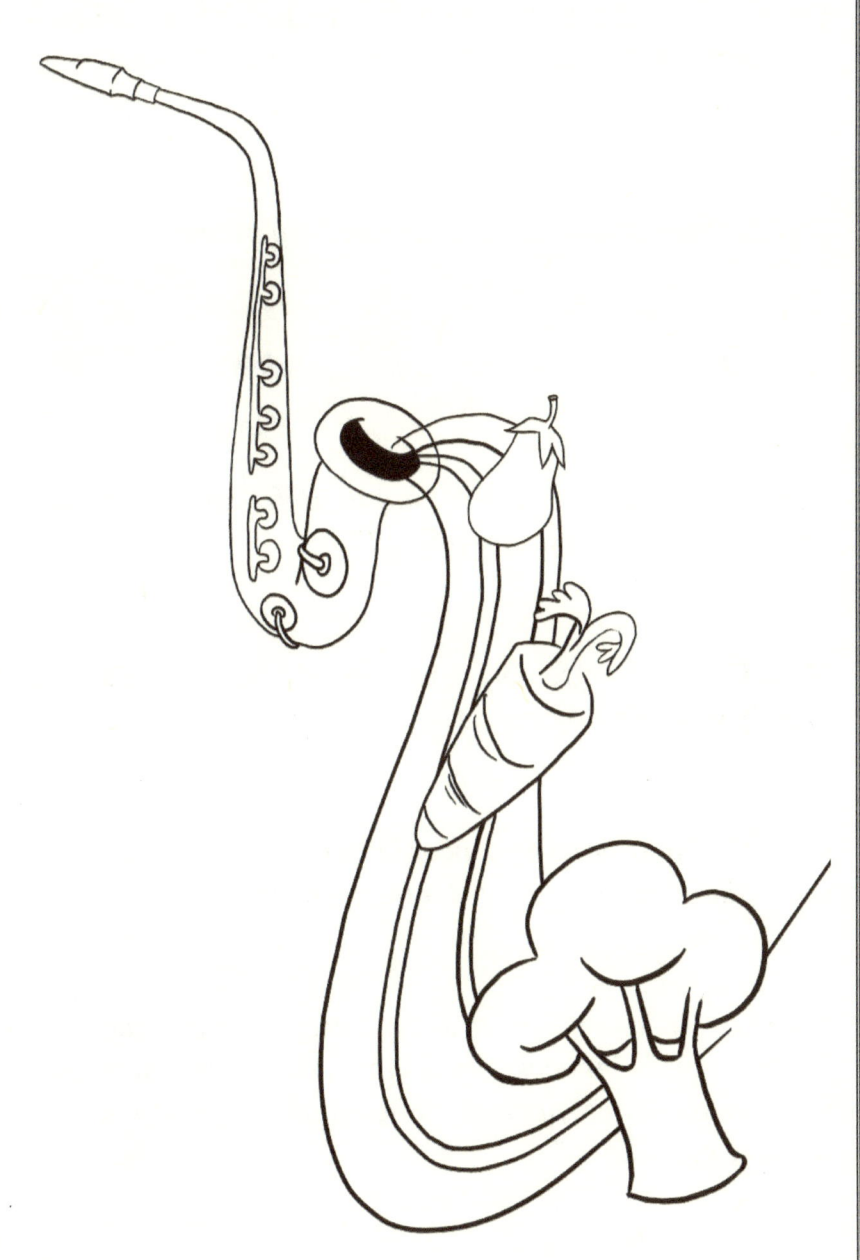

Freddy was telling his friend that he had been having some trouble sleeping. Gary asked him what he thought was the problem.

Freddy: *"My dog is dancing around my pillow."*

Gary: *"I thought your dog stayed outside?"*

Freddy: *"He does, but him, my ex-wife, and my boss have been dancing around my pillow!"*

Now, Gary was extremely confused, and he wanted to find out exactly what Freddy meant.

Gary: *"So you have two people and a dog dancing around your pillow while you are trying to sleep?"*

Freddy: *"No, when I try to sleep, I keep thinking about things like my dog being sick, my divorce, and wanting to quit my job. So they are always dancing through my head and around my pillow."*

*There is obviously some extra space for a dance floor in his head.

Layla had been wanting to extend her sidewalk around the house. Her brother had experience with concrete, and was between jobs, so she asked him if he could do it for her. He agreed to do the work and framed the area for concrete. He decided to pour the concrete one morning when Layla was at work and her daughter, Angelica, was at school. That way, it would largely be dry by the time they arrived home. On that day, he poured the concrete and completed the finishing work. Then he decided to surprise his niece by etching her name into the concrete. When Angelica arrived home from school, her proud uncle showed her the permanent tribute that he created:

Angleica

* He must not have had the proper angle to spell her name correctly.

Before a faculty meeting, a few teachers were trading theories about the lack of attendance in their classes. That is when the conversation became interesting:

Art Teacher: *"It isn't like it was in my day; the Fluent Officer is practically non-existent."*

Spanish Teacher: *"The what officer?"*

Art Teacher: *"The Fluent Officer"*

Spanish Teacher: *"If we have a "fluent officer", then these kids should be doing much better in my class."*

*The Art Teacher's truant officer must not have cared when he skipped his English class back in his day!

Two new CPA's were happy to be finished with all the work associated with the tax deadline. They decided to celebrate with a few adult beverages at a local establishment. As they were talking, Bill confided in Damon. He mentioned that he was thinking about changing careers. Damon believed that his friend was only feeling that way because of the recent long hours. He told Bill, "You know that it is going to slow down for a while." Bill attempted to explain his true reasoning by proclaiming:

"It isn't that at all. It is that this work is so monogamous!"

*Bills's new career was not as monotonous......and neither did it affect his marriage!

Patrice and Rochelle got together for happy hour one afternoon. Rochelle asked Patrice how her retired in-laws were doing. Patrice assured her friend that they were doing well and continued with this:

"Steve finally finished refurnishing his car."

* I can't help but wonder if he put a new love seat in the back.

** It is not known if it was a refurbished love seat.

Two friends were talking during lunch, when one of them remembered something she wanted to tell the other. She said that her niece had lost a lot of weight and looked fantastic. Her curious friend asked how the niece had accomplished the weight loss. The proud aunt proclaimed:

"She went on the Circle K diet"

*Circle K is a chain of convenient stores, so I must wonder if she was only eating 2/$0.99 corndogs or burritos. It sounds better than eating cereal all day.

A guy met a girl at a bar one night, and they went on a date the following week. He decided that he wasn't interested in pursuing a long term relationship. Although he communicated that to her, she continued to call him. A few weeks later, he was describing the situation to his friend. He explained that he was honest with her, but:

"...she is possessed with me!"

*I guess that is one way to make someone become obsessed with you.

**I am not sure that is the friend that you would want to introduce to your sister.

A lady, from Texas, took some time from work to go visit her sister, who lived in California. On that Sunday, the Texan woke up early to get ready for her beloved Dallas Cowboys game. Her sister came into the living room and offered protests to watching the Dallas Cowboys. The debate continued from there:

Texan: *"The Cowboys are my favorite team! Do you even like football?"*

Sister: *"I watch football every Sunday, and the best team is the Forty-Liners!"*

* It sounds to me that the sister likes slot machines more than she likes football.

Becky was on her way to a staff meeting, where her boss stopped her and asked her to prepare some reports. The meeting seemed to drag on, and all that she could think about was getting started on the new assignment. After the meeting completed, her co-worker, Ted, attempted to start a casual conversation. Becky didn't want to be rude, but she wanted to get working on those reports. She apologized to Ted and told him:

"I have these reports to do, and I want to get the egg rolling!"

*It doesn't sound like that task is going to roll along very smoothly.

Jack was talking to his staff about increasing their department's profitability. He urged them to share any ideas that they felt would be useful. Jack explained that he was open to taking on any kind of challenge, as long as it leads them to being more profitable. He asked for the input and added:

"We will hold no bars in getting this accomplished."

* Surely he meant that there will be "no holds barred", and they will do whatever is legally possible!

** Hopefully, he didn't mean that they will try anything and plan on not getting caught.

A husband and wife invited a few other couples to their home to watch a highly anticipated basketball game. It was an exciting game that came down to the last shot. Everyone enjoyed the contest and immediately began recounting some of the biggest moments. Eager to be part of the excitement, one woman commented:

"That was a real nail-bedder!"

Her Husband: *"You mean a real nail-biter."*

Wife: *"How can someone bite their nails during the game? But, squeezing the ball to tightly can hurt their nail beds."*

* Maybe all basketball players should consider weekly manicures!

I was looking online to find the start time for a local high school football game. I came upon a message board where fans of the rivals were debating which team was better. Thinking that I would find the game time, I read through some of it. It was the usual biased banter until I found:

"You guys may have the physical tradition some years, but we always have the mental tradition!"

* Was he trying to say that his team would win because their motto is "I think I can, I think I can", or are the team's fans traditionally mental?

A woman took a defensive driving course and told this story from her experience. She said that it was full of "big tough looking biker dudes, with a lot tattoos". One of those guys felt compelled to tell the rest of the class about his friend. A friend who had ridden his motorcycle without a helmet and had a bad accident one night. He described his friend as thoughtful and intelligent, and then stated:

"Now, after his accident, he is just a cabbage!"

A couple of sisters were having a girl's night at one of their homes. They began telling stories about funny things that had happened at their respective workplaces. Eager to tell one of her stories, Deana proclaimed that she had one better than them all. With everyone's attention, she suddenly had nothing to say. One of her sisters implored that she tell them the story. Deana admitted:

"I can't remember what I was going to say. It is on the tip of my head!"

* I cannot confirm that the night's activities included watching the movie "Coneheads".

A lady of particularly small stature was remembering stories from her youth. She told how her uncle used to race horses, and that he used her as a rider during training. She recalled that they did not have a saddle to use. When asked how she was able to stay on the horse, she explained:

"I had to hold onto the mange."

* Riding bareback doesn't sound to fun, especially if the horses had the mange.

After church one Sunday afternoon, a man walked into his mother-in-law's house. He spotted his brother-in-law sitting at the kitchen table, and asked "Hey, what are you up to?" As the brother-in-law was eyeing a circular, he replied:

"Ah, nothing. I am just window shopping."

* How much would you pay for a window into his world?

Alfonzo was telling a small group about the shoulder pain that he had been experiencing. Of course, there was a variety of suggestions on how to manage the pain. Johnny's wisdom led him to propose that a visit to a doctor might be a good idea. Alfonzo shrugged off that suggestion saying :

"They are just going to want to do surgery!"

Johnny asked why that would be a problem if he really needed his shoulder surgically repaired. Alfonzo echoed his feelings that he did not want to have surgery by responding:

"I don't want them to put me out under the table!"

*It certainly would be a more complex surgery if he was under the table.

A couple attended a party where they encountered one of the husband's old classmates. The woman was updating the them about a female classmate who she had run into recently. She told them how the lady was widowed and raising her kids while working two jobs. She was so impressed that she told them:

"I appraise her for that."

The wife asked "You appraise her?"

The lady confidently answered:

"I absolutely appraise her!"

* My appraisal for a woman with that type of dedication would also be high. Probably high enough to say that I applaud her for that.

Shelly use to work at a bank that gave out calendars to their customers. One year, the calendar featured a different recipe each month. At a family gathering, Shelly took some calendars to give to everyone. Her niece was thumbing through the calendar, when a particular recipe caught her eye. The niece turned to her mother and exclaimed:

"I want to try this one. It seems easy, and all you would really need to get is....

.....chicken breast

.....soy sauce

.....and some semen seed."

* I am not sure that I would want to try that one. For the record, the recipe called for sesame seed.

At a wedding reception, everyone was having a good time, and many people were dancing. During the band's intermission, one little boy stayed on the dance floor showing his moves without any music. A person, at our table, commented:

"He is having so much fun that he is dancing a cappella."

Ollie had been at a party for a while, and his inhibitions were long gone. He was all over the dance floor. He took a break from dancing to get another drink, and someone sarcastically complimented his dancing. According to Ollie, his quickness is what made him a good dancer. He proclaimed:

"I am so fast that I don't two-step, I one and a half step!"

* Wouldn't that actually mean that you are slower than someone two-stepping?

At a training meeting, the speaker was discussing customer service. He spoke about treating everyone as an individual. He wanted to make the point that every customer has different circumstances and should be treated accordingly. He concluded with:

"No matter what we think about them, let's be remindful of each person."

* Someone should be reminded to invite a different speaker next time.

A local weatherman was reporting on an early cold front coming to the area. He reassured the audience that it would not last very long. As he transitioned to the projections for the next week, he warned:

"It will be comfortable the first half of the week, but then we will get another cup of cool air pouring on us."

Some family members were upset at the actions of one of their siblings. They were recounting all the bad things that they thought he had done. One of the compassionate siblings attempted to tame the conversation when she interjected:

"Everyone makes mistakes, but we shouldn't burn him a steak for it!"

* It is a shame to burn a good piece of meat, but I guess it beats having your reputation "burned at the stake".

A couple of local politicians were entrenched in a heated debate over the direction of a pending city project. One of the men voiced a point that drew a reaction from the crowd. Sensing a need to reply strongly, the other politician started by exclaiming:

"That is a mute point because......."

*How can you audibly make a mute point?

**I guess that it is a moot point, but wouldn't it be nice if we could mute all political ads!

Coming home from a road trip, a couple had a blowout. They pulled to the side of the highway, and the husband prepared to change the tire. He put out some road flares and asked his wife to get him the flashlight. She was unable to find the flashlight, so she asked for a clue. Her husband suggested that she....

"...check the glove department"

*You could probably find some good work gloves in that department, but I would guess that the flashlight would be in the glove compartment.

Lloyd was a part of a group of parents that took their kids to a science museum. Later, he was telling his friend, Tommy, about the experience:

Lloyd: *"I couldn't get my kids away from the mirror maze."*

Tommy: *"Those are fun. Did you try it?"*

Lloyd: *"Yes, but I didn't like it. Everywhere you turned, there was an optical delusion!"*

* I am sure that it would present optical illusions, but surely it isn't enough to make someone delusional.

A news reporter was on the scene of an accident where one of the vehicles caught on fire. An unidentified man had helped a woman and child out of their burning car. Fortunately, no one was seriously injured, and the story became about a heroic man's actions. The station aired the story, which included these words from the reporter:

"*A tragedy was averted because of the quick actions of one very violent man.*"

* Violent? - Did the man jerk them out of the car by their hair?

Either way, his actions to save them were valiant.

During a business meeting, the sales manager was trying to energize the new charges. He was discussing self-motivation and comparing it to an inner fire. His impassioned plea went partly like this:

"...Keep putting kindle on your fire. Use a promotion as kindle, or providing for your family as kindle. Whatever motivates you; use it as kindle and stoke that inner fire."

* I am sure that you can download an app that will put a nice fire on your electronic device, but I am not sure that was the type of kindling that he had in mind.

**If you are reading this on your Kindle, then I hope that you are not tempted to burn it.

One evening Daniel was visiting a client in an assisted living facility. The client pointed to his radio and asked Daniel to "higher it up". There was a shelf right above the radio. Daniel began moving stuff around on the shelf so that he could put the radio up there. When he finished, Daniel asked the man if that was better, which the man replied:

"I can't hear it. Higher it up!"

A couple of brothers were telling their uncle about their most recent football game. They said that the team was pretty good and hit hard. Their father was very impressed with the other team. He told a story about when another player was hit by two opponents simultaneously. To verify the point, the father added:

"They concussioned him, Bro. They concussioned him!"

Julie went into her boss's office to give him her two week notice. She explained that her and her husband had decided to start their own business. They talked through an exit strategy, and Julie's boss was genuinely excited for her. The boss started to share some of the pitfalls that she may encounter, when she interrupted by saying:

> "I know that there is a lot of work to be desired, but I am ready for it."

*I don't know how much work anyone actually desires, but that is a trait that may help push her to success.

It was late one night, and I was trying to finish watching a movie. Then one of those extremely long and boring infomercials came on. I wasn't sure if I was going to be able to stay awake until the end of the movie, much less the end of that infomercial. Then I heard the announcer proclaim:

"Call now, and we will double size the order!"

* I don't remember the product, but were they saying that I would get a knife with a 14" blade instead of the 7" blade, or a juicer with the space to fit a whole watermelon.

**If they just doubled the order, then I could give the other one away.

A group of new employees were at a training class, when the class discussion got a little off topic. The majority of the trainees disagreed with one of their colleague's points. They bombarded him with objections about his philosophy. He tried to explain that he hadn't come to any conclusions, but was still trying to form an opinion on the subject. He eased the tension in the room, but increased the scrutiny on himself when he explained:

"I was just verbalizing it in my head."

Raymond was meeting with a potential client one afternoon. The prospect told Raymond that he wanted his wife to be involved in the decision, so he asked Raymond to meet them at their home later. They agreed on a convenient time, and the potential client began to give the address.

He told Raymond: *"3234 Bine"*

Raymond wrote *3...2...3...4...B...i*

He interrupted: *"No, Bine!"*

Raymond finished *3234 Bi...n...e, and then changed it to Byne.*

He corrected Raymond again: *"No, it is the other B"*

Raymond thought for a minute and changed it to *3234...V...ine.*

The man smiled, shook his head, and said "Yes!"

* Later, Raymond was glad to be looking for 3234 Vine!

Antonio had a bad tooth ache, and he asked his co-worker for a recommendation of a dentist. She asked him what exactly was ailing him. He told her:

"I have a capsule."

* He meant that he had a cavity.

At a family gathering on a hot summer day, Nadia decided to make snow-cones for everyone. She asked her sister what flavor she wanted. The sister's answer:

"I don't want one of those things. It will just give me a freezer head."

* A very unique way to express a reluctance to "brain freeze".

A man really wanted to get the newest cell phone, but he was worried about having to wait in a very long line on opening day. He was debating whether to go to the store, and be in a long line, or wait a day or two when the demand would dissipate. He didn't have a lot of time to wait, but they might be out of stock if he went later. He eventually decided to wait until a different day. His explanation:

"If I go now, then I probably wouldn't get one anyway because I would be at the bottom of the line."

* Was it coming out on "Black Friday", and he was worried about being stampeded?

One Saturday morning, Leon was having coffee with a group of friends. He decided to tell them that he had decided to retire early. Carl was worried about Leon having enough money to retire. Carl pulled him aside and privately voiced his concerns. Leon explained that he was going to move to the country and grow a variety of vegetables. He planned on having enough food for himself and even having some to sell at the farmer's market. Carl still wasn't convinced of the viability of the plan when Leon told him:

"Don't worry, I have a couple of green hands. I can grow anything."

*I never knew that the incredible hulk was considered a good farmer!

Rachel told me a story about going in for a job interview. It was the second interview, so there must have been a possibility of her getting hired. Rachel said during the interview, the hiring manager told her that he was concerned. Her previous employer listed her as "not eligible for rehire". Rachel explained that she had resigned, and did not plan on working there again. Out of curiosity, she asked why she was categorized as ineligible for rehire. The interviewer said that he was told:

"She does not take corrective criticism well."

She reportedly replied:

"Well who likes to get corrected all the time!"

*She actually did get the job and still works there today. Maybe her current boss opted for constructive criticism.

A lady, who was new to her leadership position, was presenting to a group of peers. The topic of her presentation was staying motivated toward success in the business. She started nervously, but continued through it. She was almost finished when she implored:

"Keep your nose to the prize......"

* I didn't know if she meant "keep your eye on the prize" or maybe the company was going to start giving scratch and sniff awards.

A group of coaches were eagerly waiting for a signed letter of intent from a talented high school player. None of the coaches had seen the letter yet, but a member of the administrative staff had seen it. She told them that there was a problem with the LOI because:

".....the letter is ineligible."

The lead recruiter worried that something had happened making the student-athlete ineligible by NCAA rules. Thankfully, it was only that the fax machine did not print it correctly, and the letter was:

"illegible"

A sales team had committed to some specific goals during a company retreat. A few months later, the management decided to reiterate the self-imposed standards. The team was reminded:

> *"We agreed to these goals, even if they were alcohol-filled."*

* Alcohol-fueled goals are one thing, but what would alcohol-filled goals look like:

-I will drink 3 beers before making sales calls, or I will only present to a prospect after buying them 2 shots of tequila.

Olivia was talking with her friends and explaining why she felt so tired. She told them that she had not slept much the night before because of terrible

"acid reflex"

She described her broken night of sleep by telling them:

"Every time I was about to fall asleep, I had another reflex!"

A couple decided to invite a bunch of their friends over for a party. After a little socializing, the men migrated to the room with the pool table, while the women remained talking in the kitchen. After a while, June took some beers in for the men. While June was delivering the bottles, one of the men let out some flatulence. Then another did the same. It was a rather unpleasant odor. June ran out of the room complaining. When she arrived back into the kitchen, the other women asked what the men were doing. Disgusted, June reported:

"They are in there throwing farts!"

*Is throwing a fart a superpower that men are finally learning to harness?

Two sisters were going on a trip. Something came up, and they got started later than they had planned. As they came into a large city, it was very slow-moving because of everyone leaving work. The driver was frustrated and told her sister:

"I knew if we didn't leave on time, then we would get stuck in traffic hour."

* Maybe "happy hour" would be a better time to drive since there wouldn't be as many vehicles on the road.

A young energetic coach was an assistant of a nationally ranked team. They were a talented team playing against a team who wasn't as good as they were. His team did not play well in the first half, even though they had the lead. So, at halftime, this coach delivered a passionate plea to the players about being more decisive. Here is part of what he said:

"You guys are not being divisive! We are much better than them, but it doesn't matter if we don't play divisively. It is up to you to determine how good you can be, and that can only happen if you play divisively!"

* Thankfully, the team performed decisively in the second half, and they won the game easily.

During a holiday basketball tournament, some parents were expressing how happy they would be when the holidays were over. An exasperated father stated that he was tired of seeing all the unrealistic Christmas programs. One mother asked "You don't like Santa Claus or flying reindeer?" He answered:

"That's okay, but what about the indomitable snowman? How can a snowman be indomitable?"

* I like that snowman. How could he have such an abominable attitude toward it?

Tracy was watching a sporting event on television when she saw her cousin in the crowd. She later used social media to post a screenshot of the cousin, with her husband, and the caption:

"......they finally made their national television day-view!"

* The game was at night, so their debut could not have been viewed during the day.

When a nationally known male figure passed away, a strange conversation happened between co-workers with neighboring cubicles.

Male Co-Worker: *"Can you believe that he died?"*

Female Co-Worker: *"Yeah, he had cancer!"*

Male Co-Worker: *"Was it in his ovaries?"*

Female Co-Worker: *"He didn't have ovaries!"*

Male Co-Worker: *"What? Did he have them taken out already?"*

For all of you dog lovers, I have seen some funny ads for dogs over the years. These are my three favorites:

Needed - A well-trained Crocker Spaniard

* Were they actually looking for someone from Spain that was a good cook?

For Sale - Damnations

* I guess all they wanted for payment was your soul!

Wanted - Young Doverman

* There was no mention of a reward for catching a juvenile delinquent from Delaware.

As a football game was ending, the analyst offered his opinion on why the favored team was going to lose:

"*They admitted too many penalties to win this game!*"

* It is difficult to win if you commit too many penalties, but if you admit to every infraction, then there is no chance of winning.

Buddy was at a conference listening to a product presentation and trying to absorb all the statistical data. The presenter, sensing that the group didn't believe the numbers, proclaimed:

"It is true. Google it up, and you will find that XYZ has performed better over the last five years."

Still feeling that his point had not been received, he decided to tell a story about a well-known investor. He asked who was familiar with the investor and said:

"Well, if you are not, then Google him up!"

* For the record, my favorite statistic is that (insert any number) percent of all statistics are made up on the spot.

** 95% of all Americans have not had the opportunity to read this book, or people would live 12% longer if they laughed just one more time per day.

During an eye exam, the eye doctor told Jeff that he needed glasses. He did not tell his wife, Kate. So, the first time he wore them, it was a surprise to her. Here is a portion of the conversation when he put them on for the first time:

Kate: *"What are those?"*

Jeff: *"Do you like them? They are my new receptacles."*

Kate: *"Receptacles huh. Well, they will be perfect for some of the trash that you look at!"*

A financial planner was meeting with some clients about their retirement plan. The couple was concerned about the value of the account dropping. The planner attempted to ease their minds and explain that the market can move up or down on a daily basis. He tried to reiterate the point with this statement:

"Remember, the market is fluctional."

* Although the market does fluctuate, his explanation wasn't very functional.

Angela, who was a new department manager, asked for advice from Joe, a manager of a different department. Her department had made an error, and she was conflicted on what to do about it. Here is a condensed version of the conversation:

Joe: *"Has the problem been fixed?"*

Angela: *"We took care of the customer, but...."*

Joe: *"Are you going to report it to the store manager?"*

Angela: *"I don't know. I am just earning the staff's trust, and I don't want to let any of them get hit by the bus!"*

* My question has to be: Is it better to be thrown under the bus or to be hit by it?

As you know, most parents think that their children are perfect little angels. When a set of parents were asked to attend a meeting with their teenage daughter's teacher, they didn't think it was anything negative. They were shocked to hear about the alleged bad behavior. As the teacher was explaining her concerns, the girl's mother interrupted with:

"I have a hard time believing that. She is a shining sample at home!"

* She sounds like she sampled some undesirable behaviors at school and was a shining example of how not to act.

When their daughters' basketball team won a tournament game, two fathers went to check the posted bracket. When they saw the upcoming match-up, one of the fathers' reaction was as follows:

"How did I know we would be versing them? We have versed them twice already and lost both games."

* I thought that they might have been in a poetry reading tournament, reading verses back and forth to each other.

Wildcats vs Bulldogs = Wildcats are playing against Bulldogs

Good vs Evil is not = Good versing Evil

A hiring manager was reviewing some resumes, when she saw something very unique. One resume stated, in part, that the person's experience included:

".....supervised eight insubordinates."

* If the people he supervised were insubordinate, then maybe that is why he was looking for somewhere else to work.

I stopped by a friend's office to see how his business was going. He told me that they had been very busy. He informed me that they were shorthanded because Rita was out, and he did not know when she would return. When I asked what had happened, he laughed and pulled up an e-mail for me to read. It was from one of the Rita's co-workers to the rest of the office. The e-mail read in part:

"Rita will be out at least for the rest of the week. She has been hospitalized with ammonia!"

* I had to ask if Rita had pneumonia, or if she got sick disinfecting her office?

Nigel, a regional sales manager, was helping an office manager plan the build-out of a new office. He was determined to make sure that the office manager understood his authority and recognized his expertise. He routinely shot down any of the office manager's ideas. The biggest point of contention was where and how the work stations were to be set up. Nigel wanted an open floor plan and emphatically stated:

"All the cuticles should be in the open. That way, you can see if people are actually working in the cuticle, or if they are wasting time in the cuticle."

*I feel like the only thing Nigel wanted is for everyone to work their fingers to the bone.

A news station was reporting breaking news that state troopers were conducting an investigation into corrupt city officials. The reporter on the scene disclosed which positions were under fire, which included:

"…..the mayor, police chief, and the intern city manager."

*That is a nice internship (city manager). I wonder if it pays the same as being the interim city manager!

Two friends were sitting at a bar talking about their upcoming dates. Curt told Jason that he was going to have dinner with Linda. Linda was a good friend of Jason's ex-girlfriend, and Jason didn't care too much for her. Curt asked Jason if he had a problem with him dating Linda. Jason answered:

"You are the one taking her out, so whatever floats to the top."

* Did he dislike her so much that he compared her to a floater, or maybe he meant whatever floats your boat?

A couple of business partners agreed that they needed to promote some interns to full-time, for their growing business. Harry thought that Amy would be a good candidate. Here is how the discussion went:

Harry: *"Have you done any projects with Amy?"*

Richard: *"Not yet; Do you think that she can get the job done?"*

Harry: *"She has been great. She works hard and is as smart as a tack."*

Richard: *"So, she works hard, but isn't very smart?"*

Harry: *"No, she definitely knows the job."*

Richard: *"Tacks aren't smart, but if she is good, then let's bring her on full-time.*

Harry: *"I know that you'll like her, she is as sharp as a whip."*

Debra was venting about what she called "the new rich". She was referring to people that quickly come into large sums of money. She was frustrated by the ones who aren't responsible with the windfall. Her example:

"Like the people that get a big inheritance and run out of money in a year or two. They end up with nothing because they just go on shopping exertions!"

* I don't ever recall expending too much energy on any shopping excursions.

One of our friends was telling us a story about something funny that her daughter did. It was a funny story, but the disclosure of her own reaction was even better. She actually told us:

"I laughed so hard that tears were running down my pants."

Barry and Claire were interested in buying a house. They were out for a drive when they saw a nice home with a "for sale" sign in the yard. There was a lady cutting the yard so they decided to stop. Barry asked the woman if she owned the home, which she verified. He then asked her how many bedrooms it had. She responded by saying:

"Call the sign!"

He then inquired about the asking price, and she repeated:

"Call the sign!"

* I am not sure if the sign had more intellect than the homeowner, but I am pretty sure it had a better personality.

Two friends were on their way to a business meeting, when Will asked Markus about his kids. His oldest was preparing to graduate from high school. Markus couldn't believe that she would be leaving for college soon. He began to reminisce about when she was younger, and he started to become emotional. He wanted to change the subject and attempted to do so by saying:

"I don't want to get nostalgia on you."

* Will probably wouldn't get nostalgic about getting any on him.

Lynn ran into Elizabeth at work one early Monday morning. They began discussing how each of their weekends had gone. Elizabeth's weekend was nice, but she was disappointed in how her favorite pro football team had performed. That was Lynn's favorite team as well, but she was more concerned with the injury that the quarterback sustained. She asked Elizabeth:

"Did you know he broke his cervical?"

* I am not a doctor, but I am pretty sure that it was a broken clavicle!

Nick and Jackson used to work for the same company. That was before Jackson decided to leave and start his own company. After a few months, Nick called to see how the new venture was going. Jackson declared:

"It was tough in the beginning, but worth it. I have been able to get it started because I detained some of my old clients."

* I hope that they weren't detained for something illegal, because he wouldn't be able to retain his reputation.

Belinda was organizing a company picnic. She had placed Ruben in charge of cooking. Belinda asked Ruben what he was planning for the meal. He told her that he was going to grill some sausage, ribs, and fajitas. Linda was excited about the selection and exclaimed:

"Fajitas are my favorite, especially when they are marmaladed just right!"

* I have never put preserves on fajitas, but I think that I will just stick to traditional marinades.

A group of friends went to watch a football game, and the band started playing during a time out. An enthusiastic lady began to dance, and then her adult daughter proclaimed:

"Hey mom, you should be on Dancing in the Stars!"

Isn't it annoying when you hear a song, and you get stuck humming or singing it all day. Think about this the next time it happens, and maybe it won't be so difficult.

Melissa was telling us that she watches the same animated movie with her kids every night. The previous night was no different, and now she had been singing the theme song all day. She was aggravated and said:

> "That song keeps resigning in my head."

* The thought that kept resonating in my head was "Just let that song resign and move on to something else,"

Three friends were spending the day shopping together. They decided to have lunch before they went to the next store. Two of the ladies had differing opinions on where to have lunch. They decided to let the third woman be the deciding vote. When asked, the third woman responded:

"I am mutual"

At that point, the other two women asked "Your feelings are mutual with which one of us?"

She replied:

"I don't want to pick between you two, so I am mutual."

They figured out that she meant neutral.

* All women want a friend to shop with that has mutual feelings about their purchases.

** All the men reading this are extremely happy that they don't go shopping with their friends.

Jennifer asked her friend Norma to join her for drinks after a particularly long day at work. As they settled in, Jennifer began to vent about a woman who was making her job difficult. She was dependent on a report that the woman did not complete, and there was no way that Jennifer could adequately finish her tasks. Norma advised her to tell her boss the entire situation. Jennifer assured her that she had, but her co-worker....

"…….denied it to the T."

* I wonder if her Long Island Tea contributed to Jennifer failing to describe the situation "to a T".

Kristi and Bart had just moved into a new area. Kristi thought that having a party was a good way to get to know the neighbors. Bart figured that having everyone over for the game would be perfect. Before the game started, one of the ladies asked Kristi who she wanted to win. Kristi nonchalantly answered:

"It doesn't matter to me, but Bart likes the Cornhustlers."

* Would that be a rogue version of the Nebraska Cornhuskers?

A basketball coach was excited about his player's first half productivity. He enthusiastically announced:

"If you keep this up, then you'll break history!"

* It must have been one powerful performance!

A young man had been looking for work for quite some time. He was thrilled when he found a job, even if it was only a temporary assignment. He told his mom, whom he lived with, that he found a job in linguistics. She was excited for him. She was also feeling sad that he would have to move away for a while, since she was unaware of any linguistics companies in their town.

She asked: *"How long will you be gone?"*

He answered: *"At least eight hours a day."*

Mom: *"I figured as much, but when will you be back in town?"*

Son: *"I am not leaving town!"*

Mom: *"What company hired you?"*

Son: *"Duh, UPS. Haven't you seen the commercial? We are linguistics!"*

Mom: *"Good luck!"*

* What can Brown do for you? They can start by teaching the young man the difference between logistics and linguistics.

During a sales meeting, Bill was once again named "Salesperson of the Month". Bertha was astounded, and she wondered how he repeatedly earned that honor. She exclaimed:

"He must have a sick sense or something!"

* I don't think he won the award by knowing when he would be sick, but my sixth sense is telling me that Bill will win the award again.

Veronica was counting down the days until her retirement. Trish worked with Veronica and asked how many days were left before her retirement. After receiving an answer, Trish asked what excited her the most about retiring.

Veronica quickly answered:

"I won't have to listen to the band playing so loudly in the morning!"

Trish knew that Veronica lived near a school, so she inquired:

"Does the band practice that early in the morning?"

Veronica was puzzled by the question and explained:

"They don't need to practice. They are already playing on my radio!"

* She had described her alarm going off as "the band playing"!

Felicia was putting together a lunchtime mixer for local business owners. Her assistant was helping organize the event, and she had made a list of things they needed. Going through the list late one night, Felicia noticed a strange entry:

"Luncheon Meets"

The next day, Felicia explained that she intended to get sandwich trays instead of a bunch of lunch meat. She was surprised when her assistant clarified the listing:

"I wasn't talking about the food. I meant that we need to solidify a way that everyone gets to meet everyone else at the luncheon."

*So, if you want your business to thrive, then stock up on luncheon meets!

Paul was telling stories of his football playing days back in college. He was making an effort to declare that the players, when he played, were tougher than the present versions. He began to describe a particular violent hit to one of his teammates. The story progressed to Paul telling us that his teammate "took some smelling sauce" and went right back in the game. Paul made sure we understood his point and reiterated:

"He took the smelling sauce and didn't miss another play!"

*I don't know what kind of "sauce" it was, but I am sure it would be a banned substance in today's game. I am not even sure they use "smelling salts" anymore.

Kendal was presenting a business opportunity to a small group. He was discussing the numerous activities that would be required to be successful. Kendal wanted everyone to be clear that many of those activities would overlap, so he attempted to explain it by stating:

"You are going to have a lot of plates in the air."

After that example, he wanted to reveal the secret to success in the business:

"How you balance those plates will determine how successful you will be."

*Juggling tennis balls is simple compared to balancing plates in mid-air.

Many sporting events make use of the baseball vernacular "on deck" and "in the hole". "On deck" refers to the next in line, while the one after that is considered "in the hole". Field events at track meets are good examples. At a high school track meet, I heard an interesting adaptation. The person running the pole vault event constantly communicated the next three competitors. She authoritatively announced:

"Michael is up, Javier is on deck, and Anthony is on hold."

I laughed after hearing it the first time, but she never corrected it throughout the entire two-hour competition.

*Michael is up, Javier is on deck, and Anthony is on hold. Would someone please pick up the phone and see what Anthony wants?

A company's management team decided to increase the minimum requirements expected from the team members. There were a number of employees who immediately questioned the changes. A representative, from the main office, met with a group of employees and sternly stated:

"These changes are not dictionary!"

* They were right. You couldn't find a good reason for the changes in the dictionary, whether the changes were discretionary or not."

Nikki and Ralph, a newly married couple, were having a debate. Neither one could understand why the other didn't understand their own point of view. Ralph continued to try to convince her when she told him:

"I just don't agree with you."

That statement led Ralph to retort:

"Well, I agree with myself!"

* If you need someone to agree with you, then yourself is not a bad place to start.

Owen went on a date one night. A few days later, his curious sisters kept hassling him about the date. To get them off of his back, he told them:

"Don't worry about it. She was just a nightstand!"

* I guess that he was just looking for someone to hold a lamp or his alarm clock.

A young lady went to her mother's house to have the mom braid her hair. Her mother was glad to help and excited to have her over for a visit. After a while, the daughter grabbed a mirror to check the progress. She wasn't satisfied with the results, and asked her to fix it. When her mother asked what was wrong with it, the daughter exclaimed:

"My crack is crooked!"

*She meant that that part was crooked.

As Roxanne was leaving the office for an afternoon appointment, she ran into an associate in the lobby. She updated him on a particular client's situation, and told him that she just wanted to keep him in the loop. The office assistant had just finished a phone call, and interjected:

"What am I........chopped onions?"

After chuckling, Roxanne asked *"Do you mean chopped liver?"*

The assistant's response:

"No, I like liver, but chopped onions make my eyes water."

* Touché

During a sports highlight show, the announcer explained why a key player didn't play the majority of the game:

"He was rejected from the game."

* It can't be fun to be ejected from a game, but it has to be tough being rejected by the game that he loves.

A woman went through a tough break-up, and she wasn't feeling very good about herself. A friend wanted to be supportive and told her multiple times:

'You are a very prettyful girl!"

* Would this actually be considered a compliment? I guess that it depends on what you are pretty full of.

Chloe had recently gone to her high school reunion. Of course, she posted all about the events on social media. She reported that she had won the reward for being married the longest, and another won the reward for traveling the farthest to attend. And so, it continued on like that:

...the reward for most spouses...

...the reward for longest career...

...the reward for least amount of gray hair...

* Where did they graduate from? .....Alcatraz?

A basketball player endured a gruesome injury during a big game. As the production crew was preparing to show the replay, the audience was warned:

"This is not for the fair at heart!"

During a baseball game, the shortstop fumbled the ball around before making the throw to first for the out. As they were showing the replay, the broadcaster described the unusual play by saying:

"He kind of gave it the half double-clutch"

*Hmm....did he clutch once or was his movement only half of a normal "double-clutch".

Brandt received a call one afternoon asking for his help. The person was having problems getting their last paycheck from a previous employer. In this manner, the caller explained how they avoided paying:

"They just keep giving me the ride around!"

*No, he did not work with the police department.

At a family barbeque, the cook was preparing the grill. He asked his wife to bring the meat out for him. When she delivered the meat, she asked if there was anything else that he needed. He already had a spatula, but answered:

"You can bring me some thongs."

It didn't stop there. One of the kids asked him what thongs were. His reply:

"I can handle the hot dogs easier with the thongs."

* Thankfully, his wife brought out a grilling tool (tongs) and not something else for him to wear under his apron.

If you have ever taken a road trip, then you have probably seen cars being towed to a new destination. The trail car will display a warning that the vehicle is "In Tow". That warning is usually made from duct or masking tape. In South Texas, we get to see various versions of these warnings. Here are a couple of my favorites:

"In Town"

* Are they telling us the origin or the destination?

How about this one:

"In Toe"

* I spell it "Tow", they spell it "Toe"; let's just call the whole thing off.

At a home owners' association meeting, some of the members were voicing their complaints. Janet was extremely frustrated with her neighbor's teenage son. According to her, the boy constantly had his music up loud and drove recklessly through the neighborhood. To accentuate her point, she claimed:

"Last night, he threw his rubber on the ground!"

* After investigating, the HOA officers found that there had been no littering, but there were tire tracks in front of the young driver's home.

I am sure medical professionals have heard this mentioned plenty of times. After a doctor's appointment, a man called his wife with the diagnosis. The man told his wife that he needed surgery to repair his:

"rotator cup"

* It is probably difficult to even pick up a cup with a torn rotator cuff.

* A post route, in football, is when the wide receiver runs down the field and suddenly adjust his path at a forty-five degree angle, hypothetically toward the goal post.

Nathan was a proud father who had been teaching his sons the game of football. They gathered in an open field to play a pick-up game with many of their friends. They split the teams evenly, and Nathan played quarterback for both teams. After misconnecting on a couple of passes, Nathan told one of his sons:

"Just run a pole route."

* Maybe it was a punishment. Countless middle school football players have been commanded to run to the pole and back.

A weather reporter came on television and began discussing the major snow storm that hit the area. She described the road conditions and issued this warning:

"Be careful on the roads tomorrow because there will be even more implement weather!"

* Was she saying that driving a combine was the only safe way to drive in the inclement weather?

Cindy really likes ice cream, and she eats a portion almost every night. David, her loving husband, asked her if she wanted him to get some for her. She requested ice cream in a cone, and here is what was said next:

David: *"What kind would you like tonight?"*

Cindy: *"I think that I would like the Napoleon."*

David: *"With my metabolism, even Neapolitan ice cream would be my Waterloo!"*

Donna and Gail were friends whose husbands traveled a lot for their jobs. They began discussing where their husbands were working that week:

Donna: *"Where is George this week?"*

Gail: *"Massa-two-shits"*

Donna: *"You mean Massachusetts?"*

Gail: *"He is in Boston!"*

* It was apparent that Gail couldn't give two s...s where George was as long as he made money.

A father was trying to relate to a couple of his sons. Those two boys were into trading baseball cards at the time. The father attempted to show his baseball acumen, when he told them:

"The Horge (h-ohr-j) Bell card is a good one!"

The player's name was Jorge Bell, pronounced George.

* If you were going to pronounce the "J" with a "H" sound, wouldn't it sound more like h-or-hay?

**I am glad that the father wasn't their Spanish tutor!

Kim had a list of all the tasks that she needed to complete at work that day. She was making some progress and marking things off of her list. She came to one, that wasn't a priority, and said to no one in particular:

"I'll put that one on the burner in the back."

* I guess when it came to learning new idioms, she put that one on the back burner.

A professional athlete made a crucial mistake at the end of a game. His team ended up losing, and he was going to take the blame. In the post-game interview, the player struggled to find the proper words to explain what happened. He exhaled and admitted:

"It's a humbling piece of the pie."

*Those who have been on a diet know that any piece of pie is humbling.

Mandy had some complaints about how new management was handling her apartment community. She went to the office to make those concerns known. She began by asking why the office no longer would receive packages for tenants not at home during attempted delivery. The answer confused her:

> "The corporate office made that decision during the remodelization."

Mandy wasn't really sure what that meant, but she decided to move to the next issue. She was concerned that the gate didn't work and that anyone could enter the property. The office manager's answer still didn't help:

> "That will be part of the ongoing remodilization. The remodelization won't be completed overnight."

*That corporation should think about renovating their staff even before the remodeling is complete.

Max, a contractor, had instructed a painting crew to paint an accent stripe in one of the rooms. When he arrived at the location, he immediately saw a problem. The stripe was only painted three-quarters of the way across the wall. Max contacted Steve, the painter, to inquire why it hadn't been finished. Steve explained that they didn't have enough tape for the entire length of the wall. That is when the conversation really became interesting:

Max: *"Can you get it finished by the end of the day?"*

Steve: *"It's already finished!"*

Max: *"The stripe is to be painted across the whole wall"*

Steve: *"We didn't have enough tape to do the whole wall."*

Max: *"The stripe is supposed to go to the end of the wall. That is just common sense!"*

Steve: *"Well, my common sense is different than your common sense!"*

*This book proves that common sense isn't as common as it should be.

Bonus Stories

On the night before Christmas, two brothers (Lenny and Jay) discussed going fishing. Lenny had come in from out of town, and his wife and kids were taking the rental car back to the hotel. After fishing, Lenny would need a ride back to the hotel. Jay made a deal with his brother. Jay would take him back to the hotel as long as Lenny promised to buy him a Whataburger.

It was set, and the brothers were off on their fishing adventure. Later, on the way to the hotel, Jay was ready to cash in and get his desired hamburger. Lenny didn't mind keeping his end of the bargain, but there was a problem that they didn't think about. It was Christmas Eve, and all the Whataburger restaurants were closed. Jay was disappointed. He delivered his brother, went home, and fell asleep thinking about that juicy Whataburger.

The next day, the whole family came together for Christmas dinner. Everyone was enjoying each other's company, when someone noticed a big bruise on Jay's wife's arm. When asked what happened, she simply stated "Jay bit me". He had been thinking so much about missing out on the Whataburger that he dreamt about having one. During his dream, he grabbed his wife's arm, thinking it was a tasty hamburger, and took a bite. She immediately pulled away and yelled at him, but it still left a bruise and teeth marks that were visible the next afternoon.

My wife is 4'10" (4' 10 1/2", if you ask her), and she weighs a bit over 100 pounds. We had been visiting my family, and I took her to Churchill Downs for the first time. It was a nice warm day, and there were a lot of people at the races.

I told her to stay close as we maneuvered through the crowd. We took some time to explore and then made our way to the paddock. I thought that she would enjoy seeing the horses up close, but she was clutched onto my side. I asked if she was alright, and she responded "You told me to stay close!" I explained "I just didn't want them to put you on a horse thinking you were a jockey."

*Of course, I took a well-deserved elbow to the ribs.

Two brothers, Larry and Donnie, both lived in a town four hours from their nearest relatives. They had a good relationship and a healthy sibling rivalry. With one being a former Marine and the other serving in the Air Force, they enjoyed constantly ribbing each other. Their sisters also got into the act, commonly referring to the brothers as "the ugly sisters".

Larry had gotten to the age where it was time for the dreaded prostate exam. Reluctantly, he scheduled the appointment, which came faster than he hoped. Of course, Donnie wasn't going to let him forget about his upcoming intimate experience. On that inevitable day, none of the sisters had heard from Larry. That afternoon, one of the sisters called Donnie to see if he knew how Larry was doing. With a serious voice, Donnie told her "I think he enjoyed it because he is going back for a second opinion."

*To be clear, everything was fine, and the second opinion was not needed, nor desired.

Acknowledgements

Thank you to all of the relative geniuses who have brought smiles to our faces and joy to our ordinary days.

To my wife, Nora, for helping me gather many of the stories and your unrelenting support through the process.

Illustrations inside the book were created by Erik Sanchez.

Cover design by Killer Book Covers.

www.killerbookcovers.com

Formatting and Interior Design by Suzette Vaughn

www.suzettevaughn.com

About the Author

Ron Lang is a well traveled and experienced coach and entrepreneur. His journeys have revealed the unique quirks of people in many regions of the U.S. Ron lives with his wife, Nora, and they still compile fun examples of relative genius. He is dedicated to authoring books that deliver stories of wonderful people, great experiences, and a lot of fun. Ron is currently working on his next project, which is sure to bring more positivity and inspiration into your life.

If you have enjoyed this book, then please tell a friend (or two), leave a review on Amazon, and search for Ron's other published works.

www.ingramcontent.com/pod-product-compliance
Lightning Source LLC
Chambersburg PA
CBHW020413080526
44584CB00014B/1308